100
CLASSIC
BOOKS
About Higher Education

A Compendium and Essays

Cameron Fincher, George Keller,
E. Grady Bogue, and John R. Thelin

Phi Delta Kappa Educational Foundation
Bloomington, Indiana U.S.A.

Cover design by
Victoria Voelker

Phi Delta Kappa Educational Foundation
408 North Union Street
Post Office Box 789
Bloomington, Indiana 47402-0789
U.S.A.

Printed in the United States of America

Library of Congress Catalog Card Number 2001090103
ISBN 0-87367-833-8

Table of Contents

Introduction
by George Keller

This slight publication by four long-time students of higher education lists what we regard as 100 of the most important and influential books about U.S. colleges and universities in the 20th century. As that century ended, we thought such a list might be instructive for readers and students interested in colleges and universities, which a growing number of persons believe are the new central institutions of our increasingly knowledge-based society.

We undertook the task with fear and trembling. While some magazines like to list the 10, 20, or 50 best restaurants, films, physicians, beaches, or websites, some professors have been scathing about any attempts to assemble what they label a "canon," or a body of greats sanctioned by some authority. We four are sensitive souls, so we twitched. We definitely are not a clique trying to foist a canon that reflects our own gender, class, and special discernment on the public. We merely believe that a fairly comprehensive reading list of significant works on an important topic can be of help.

Also, when we assembled our lists separately, we found that we each had 136 or 165 books on our menu. Which books could we scratch, and why? And why the metric of 100? Well, there was the parallel between the 100 years of the century and 100 books. But wasn't that arbitrary? Sure it was, but one has to make choices in life, usually without clear moral or academic authority.

There also was the fear of chauvinism. What about the major works from Germany, Mexico, or Japan? Or Israel and Sweden? In recent years centers for study of higher education have sprouted in Australia, England, France, the Netherlands, and other nations. Our lack of knowledge about foreign universities and the scholarship of other nations forced us to concentrate on books by Americans. We regret our insularity. We did, however, include the works of several European authors whose books have made an impression among many U.S. readers curious about higher education. But readers will not find books by the likes of Tony Becher, Pierre Bourdieu, Torsten Husén, Guy Neave, Johan Olsen, Ulrich Teichler, Alain Touraine, and Gareth Williams here. A particularly sad omission for us were the perceptive books written by Joseph Ben-David in the 1960s and 1970s.

What really set us quivering was the definition of a "classic." Is a classic about higher education a book that has great impact in its decade? Or a work of lasting significance? A work of great scholarship about important issues? A text with unusually elegant prose or powerful logic? Or a book of eye-opening wisdom about life and higher learning? What criteria should we use in deciding whether to include a book on our list?

We recalled how the Italian novelist Italo Calvino wrestled with the definition in the first chapter of his book, *Why Read the Classics?* He offered 14 ingredients, such as a book "which exerts a particular influence," "a work which relegates the noise of the present to a background hum," and "a book to which you cannot remain indifferent, and which helps you define yourself in relation or even in opposition to it." Calvino, like many others, also includes in his definition that a classic is a book that one returns to reread. Clearly, what makes a classic book is not a settled issue.

Rather than risk our friendships, we eclectically used some of each of the standards. We included those books that in one way or another had a significant effect on the public understanding about higher education during the past century. It's a waffling criterion, we confess, but the best on which we could agree.

Even the category "higher education" made us a bit uneasy. While the United States has 3,700 accredited colleges and universities, there are twice as many proprietary "colleges" — of computer programming, paramedical professions, secretarial science, commercial art, and automobile repairs, to name a few. There has recently sprung up a small group of degree-awarding colleges, even professional schools, that deliver courses over the Internet. Then, too, there is the burgeoning world of adult and continuing higher education, even Elderhostels. Again, we had to draw a line somewhere. So we limited our list to books about traditional two-year and four-year colleges and universities.

We also decided to exclude all histories of individual institutions even though we know of several outstanding chronicles among the hundreds of celebratory histories.

Another class of books we felt compelled to leave out were the first-rate and memorable journalistic reports about colleges and universities. This was especially hard for me because I regard great journalism as history written while it is still hot and because I think the best scholarly journalists possess an eye for significant detail, are able to bring the primary campus movers to life, and can convey an almost sensual feel about a university that some dry-as-felt and quantifying scholars cannot. For example, David Boroff's penetrating, compact college portraits in his 1961 book, *Campus USA,* have never been surpassed. And James Traub's *City on a Hill* of 1994 not only offers us a vivid picture of the City College of New York today but also presents a brilliant, melancholy description, with scholarly data, of the hopes and nightmares of open admissions to a once extraordinary municipal university. But, once again, we had to put up some fences.

One thing that readers of this guide will notice is that most of the texts we list have been written in the second half of the 20th century. Some may charge that this is because none of us four was intellectually active in the first half of the century. But we are convinced that history will show that professorial life, the work of colleges and universities, and the role of higher education in society simply were not written about much before World War II. To be sure, there were several remarkable efforts, many of which we have included in this book. And there were evocative recollections about college life, such as Henry Seidel Canby's *Alma Mater: The Gothic Age of the American College,* and novels, such as Owen Wister's *Philosophy Four,* which we did not include. But unlike corporations, the federal government, and schools, the nation's colleges and universities and their programs were not a subject of much scrutiny or a cause for national concern until quite recently. Except for several dozen celebrative histories of individual institutions and a handful of articles and books, the prewar bookshelf of studies about what the ballooning world of higher education was doing, or should be doing, was sparse.

However, as higher education has edged closer to the core of American life, economic vitality, and cultural prowess in the past few decades, the literature, journalism, and especially the scholarship about colleges and universities has multiplied. It began seriously in the 1950s with the aid of new attention by such scholars such as R. Freeman Butts, W.H. Cowley, Merle Curti, Seymour Harris, Hugh Hawkins, Richard Hofstadter, T.R. McConnell, David Riesman, Frederick Rudolph, Richard Storr, and Logan Wilson. Now, with about 14.5 million Americans enrolling annually for one or more courses and with the quality of human resources as a primary source of a nation's wealth, health, and social harmony, the study of higher education has emerged as an important and busy sector of intellectual inquiry and analysis. As the often-prophetic sociologist Daniel Bell wrote in his book on our list:

> The university now occupies a central position in the society. Formerly its chief function was that of conserving and transmitting the intellectual traditions and cultural values of society. Now the university serves more as the center for research and innovation. Though the university once reflected the status system . . . it now determines status. . . . More so than ever before in American life, the university has become a public service institution, its resources increasingly used by government, industry, and the local communities. At the same time, because of its vastly increased financial needs, the university has itself become a "constituency," a significant claimant on the monetary powers of the government. The scientific, technical, and literary intelligentsia, most of whom are now housed in the university, has become

a significant social stratum, amounting almost to a new class of society. (Bell 1966, p. 277)

It is partly because of the new importance of higher education analysis and scholarship and the growing rigor of the field during the later decades of the past century that we compiled this list of significant books. We hope it will be useful to a wide array of people: graduate students, librarians, trustees, would-be education leaders, citizens interested in campus activities and structures, diligent public officials, and historians — also, to fledgling scholars of higher education, as we once were. We apologize that our list is skimpy on such matters as university finance, feminist and ethnic concerns, architecture, and student life and on historically black institutions and community colleges. But we found few durable scholarly works on these subjects, though some began to appear at the very end of the century. New publications, such as Marilyn Boxer's *When Women Ask the Questions: Women's Studies in America* (1998), Thomas Kane's *The Price of Admission: Rethinking How Americans Pay for College* (1999), and W. Norton Grubb's *Honored but Invisible: An Inside Look at Teaching in Community Colleges* (1999), are filling gaps in the literature of the past century.

This book was pushed into motion by Cameron Fincher, Regents Professor and Director of the Institute for Higher Education at the University of Georgia. He deserves a lion's share of the credit for seeing the idea become paper and ink. We four also had the benefit of critical appraisals of an earlier draft list from three distinguished scholars of higher education: James Hearn of the University of Minnesota, Marvin Peterson of the University of Michigan, and Patrick Terenzini of Pennsylvania State University. Their comments and suggestions helped us in the winnowing process.

Finally, please remember that these are 100 significant books about higher education as we view them. They are emphatically not *the* 100 classics. You will probably want to add several books of your own, and you may howl at a few of our selections. But we hope you will appreciate that there has been an evolving and accelerating literature about one of the most fascinating social institutions that people have ever created to enhance civilized life. To find out why many people around the world believe that American higher education, despite its shortcomings, has become one of the nation's glories, the listed volumes will provide some evidence. Quite possibly, the relatively new scholarship, fiction, commentary, and criticism of higher learning may be on its way to a glory of its own in the century ahead.

100 Classic Books About Higher Education:
An Annotated List
Arranged by Author

Ashby, Eric. *Adapting Universities to the Technological Society.*
San Francisco: Jossey-Bass, 1974.
Contains 10 essays by one of England's leading thinkers about
higher education in Europe and elsewhere. Discusses the likely
consequences of mass higher education, changing student cultures, and especially the advance of the sciences and new technology — in a prophetic way.

Astin, Alexander W. *Four Critical Years: Effects of College on
Beliefs, Attitudes and Knowledge.* San Francisco: Jossey-Bass,
1977. *What Matters in College: Four Critical Years Revisited.*
San Francisco: Jossey-Bass, 1993.
A systematic analysis of changes in undergraduates' values, attitudes, beliefs, and cognitive skills. Presents a profile of the dif-
ferential effect that types of institutions make and distinguishes
the changes associated with residential-college experience as
compared to commuter-institution experience. Includes a controversial chapter on the peculiarities of public policy and higher
education priorities since World War II.

Barzun, Jacques. *The American University: How It Runs and
Where It Is Going.* New York: Harper & Row, 1968. Reprint

with new introduction by Herbert I. London, Chicago: University of Chicago Press, 1993.
An excellent commentary on the internal incentives and operations of the university. Discusses faculty careers, student experiences, administrative structure, external relations, budgets and expenditures. These are observations, advice, and counsel of a well-known intellectual.

Bell, Daniel. *The Reforming of General Education: The Columbia College Experience in Its National Setting*. New York: Columbia University Press, 1966. Reprint, Brunswick, N.J.: Transaction, 2000.
Although the focus is on the famous general education program at Columbia, this broad and deep analysis is one of the most thorough explorations of liberal arts education of the past century. Includes new social trends affecting undergraduate learning, suggestions for reform, and "notes" on the future.

Berdahl, Robert. *Statewide Coordination of Higher Education*. Washington, D.C.: American Council on Education, 1971.
An informative discussion of how statewide coordinating agencies emerged as planning, program review/evaluation, and budgeting entities. Describes and analyzes the structures of coordinating agencies that work the difficult boundary between local institutions and their governing boards and state legislatures and governors and their role in balancing the competing calls for higher education accountability and autonomy.

Bloom, Allan. *The Closing of the American Mind*. New York: Simon & Schuster, 1987.
A rousing and controversial critique of the growing politicization of the university written by an outstanding scholar who views student protests and faculty dissent through unclouded lenses and with a special talent for detecting absurdities. Argues for a return to hard intellectual inquiry undisturbed by ideological crusades.

Bogue, E. Grady, and Saunders, Robert L. *The Evidence for Quality: Strengthening the Tests of Academic and Administrative Effectiveness.* San Francisco: Jossey-Bass, 1992.
A highly perceptive and level-headed appraisal of quality assurance in higher education through accreditation, rankings and ratings, external and internal studies, licensing, reviews, and outcome assessment. Considers the growing role of the state in quality assurance and strategies for improvement.

Bok, Derek. *Beyond the Ivory Tower: Social Responsibilities of the Modern University.* Cambridge: Harvard University Press, 1982.
Examines the obligations and necessary protections of contemporary universities now that they have taken on research for the military and corporations, advocacy for greater social justice, and an expanded variety of students. Replete with prudent advice, the book also is bold, as in its suggestion that institutions strive for ethnic and racial diversity in admissions but appoint faculty strictly on merit.

Bowen, Howard R. *Investment in Learning: The Individual and Social Value of American Higher Education.* San Francisco: Jossey-Bass, 1977. Reprint with new introduction by Cameron Fincher, New Brunswick, N.J.: Transaction, 1996.
An economist and university president presents in graceful prose the strong case for higher education as a central part of the human capital investment policy. In so doing, Bowen salvages economics from a fate as the "dismal science" to one of systematic analysis and justified optimism. Considers not only the economic returns for a national investment in higher education, but also social and cultural benefits.

Bowen, Howard R., and Schuster, Jack H. *American Professors: A National Resource Imperiled.* New York: Oxford University Press, 1985.

An analysis of U.S. faculty in the decades after the end of higher education's "golden era." Provides good data and interpretation but with sobering findings. Prolonged financial stringency for institutions has started to converge with a long-term, gradual demand for nurturing a new generation of college and university professors. Sounds a warning both to campus administrators and to current and future faculty. A recurrent theme is that the prerequisites and resources necessary to maintain a strong faculty have been stretched.

Boyer, Ernest. *College: The Undergraduate Experience in America.* New York: Harper & Row, 1987.
A companion study and complementary report to an earlier Carnegie study, *High School: A Report on Secondary Education in America.* Based on extensive site visits and interviews at a wide range of institutions offering the bachelor's degree and a survey of approximately 5,000 faculty members and 4,500 undergraduates. Explores many issues affecting the undergraduate student: curricular tensions in careerism and liberal arts, campus life, faculty rewards and renewal, governance, and assessment of education outcomes.

Brubacher, John S., and Rudy, Willis. *Higher Education in Transition: An American History, 1636-1956.* New York: Harper, 1958. *Higher Education in Transition: A History of American Colleges and Universities.* New Brunswick, N.J.: Transaction, 1997.
This comprehensive survey of three centuries of American higher education persists as a balanced, clear chronicle. Intriguing insights and courage alert readers to unconventional interpretations. For example, Brubacher and Rudy resurrect a strong case for the Scottish influence on early American higher education. Comparable fresh interpretations characterize the entire work.

Butts, R. Freeman. *The College Charts Its Course: Historical Conceptions and Current Proposals.* New York: McGraw-Hill, 1939.

A commendable overview of American higher education and curricular change up to the 1930s. Compares the plans, programs, and policies for colleges and universities and their underlying theories, focusing on key issues and controversies involving conservatives and progressives.

Buckley, William F. *God and Man at Yale: The Superstitions of Academic Freedom.* Introduction by John Chamberlain. Chicago: Regnery, 1951.
Written after his graduation from Yale, this book caused a sensation, charging that most of the university's professors scoffed at religion as superstition and advocated socialist or left-wing anti-capitalist views. It names names, lists books assigned, and charges campus presidents with spineless complicity with the secularism and anti-Americanism of elite institutions.

Caplow, Theodore, and McGee, Reece J. *The Academic Marketplace.* New York: Basic Books, 1958. Reprint, Brunswick, N.J.: Transaction, 1999.
A critical analysis and interpretation of the academic profession that focuses on faculty mobility, appointments, evaluation, and what these processes reveal about academic goals and values. Surveys with remarkable candor the filling of faculty vacancies in liberal arts departments at nine major universities from 1954 to 1956.

Carnegie Foundation for the Advancement of Teaching. *Missions of the College Curriculum: A Contemporary Review with Suggestions.* San Francisco: Jossey-Bass, 1977.
A commendable overview of college and university curricula and the need for realistic change. Offers penetrating analyses of the factors shaping curriculum in higher education and the major trends and issues in curriculum composition, development, and change. Challenging and thought-provoking but often ignored.

Carnegie Foundation for the Advancement of Teaching. *The Control of the Campus: A Report on the Governance of Higher*

Education. Princeton N.J.: Carnegie Foundation for the Advancement of Teaching, 1982.

Any report drafted by a committee runs the risk of sacrificing a distinctive point of view to achieve balance and compromise. This work is no exception. The net gain, however, is that it succeeds in providing a good primer on public policy and higher education. Chapters on courts, state governments, accreditation, federal relations, national associations, and boards of trustees are organized around themes of institutional independence, autonomy, and self-regulation.

Chickering, Arthur W. *Education and Identity.* San Francisco: Jossey-Bass, 1969. Second edition, with Linda Reisser, San Francisco: Jossey-Bass, 1993.

An outstanding interpretation of personal development as an education objective and outcome. Makes good use of theory and research in social psychology, identifies seven "major developmental vectors" (for example, achieving competence, managing emotions, developing integrity). Discusses two principles: development (as alternating cycles of differentiation and integration) and experience (as dependent on personal characteristics). Excellent references and interesting quotations.

Clark, Burton R. *The Higher Education System: Academic Organization in Cross-National Perspective.* Berkeley: University of California Press, 1983.

Discusses how higher education institutions are organized in several nations. Includes descriptions of authority, integration, society, modes of change, and belief systems, as well as a "normative theory" and the author's view that universities need loose structures and "disorder."

Clark, Burton R. *The Academic Life: Small Worlds, Different Worlds.* Princeton, N.J.: Carnegie Foundation for the Advancement of Teaching, 1987.

Brings to life the working world of professors, whether it be a snapshot of the daily round or the long-term trajectory of a career path. Combines systematic survey data with profiles of institutions and departments. The salient message is that American higher education is large, diverse, and complex — and facile generalizations about the academic life must be tempered with the particulars and peculiarities of individuals, the institution, and the discipline.

Cohen, Arthur M., and Brawer, Florence B. *The American Community College.* San Francisco: Jossey-Bass, 1982. Third edition, 1996.
The most comprehensive text on two-year colleges, with their history, structure, curricula, students, and finances described in knowledgeable detail. Points to and analyzes the four roles of these institutions (transfer, career training, community services, and remedial education) and portrays the changes taking place among them.

Cohen, Michael D., and March, James G. *Leadership and Ambiguity: The American College President.* New York: McGraw-Hill, 1974. Second edition, Boston: Harvard Business School Press, 1986.
A frequently quoted study that argues that campus presidents can do very little, that most universities are an "organized anarchy," that the "world is absurd," and that conventional models of presidential leadership in academe are mistaken. Nonetheless, the authors offer advice in how college leaders can accomplish small things if they are clever.

Corson, John J. *Governance of Colleges and Universities.* New York: McGraw-Hill, 1960. *The Governance of Colleges and Universities: Modernizing Structure and Processes.* New York: McGraw-Hill, 1975.
A highly professional look at the unique characteristics of college and university decision-making and governance processes and the responsibilities of trustees, administrators, and faculty. For a before-and-after view of the 1960s, the two books should be read as one.

Cowley, W.H. *Presidents, Professors, and Trustees: The Evolution of American Academic Government.* San Francisco: Jossey-Bass, 1980.

A collection of essays by one of the pioneers in the study of higher education and an exceptionally wise and historically grounded scholar. Traces the roots of present-day campus governance, puncturing several myths through richly detailed research.

Cross, K. Patricia. *Accent on Learning: Improving Instruction and Reshaping the Curriculum.* San Francisco: Jossey-Bass, 1976.

A candid discussion of adjusting curriculum and instruction so that all students have "the opportunity for high-level achievement" as well as open access. Identifies the new kinds of students populating colleges and universities and the "total educational experience." Addresses ways of individualizing instruction: self-paced instruction, mastery learning, and differences in learning styles.

Cross, K. Patricia. *Adults as Learners: Increasing Participation and Facilitating Learning.* San Francisco: Jossey-Bass, 1981.

An excellent overview of adult and continuing education. Addresses the possibilities of a "learning society" populated by "lifelong learners" who possess the basic skills for learning, and the motivation to pursue a variety of learning interests throughout their lives.

Dressel, Paul. *College and University Curriculum.* Berkeley: McCutchan, 1968.

A concise introduction to philosophies in curriculum development at the college/university level and to curricular trends in liberal arts, professional disciplines, and graduate study. Examines issues in curriculum design: breadth versus depth, student versus subject, knowledge versus mode of inquiry, theory versus practice. Probes curriculum review/evaluation principles and offers views on undergraduate student outcome competencies.

Dressel, Paul. *Handbook of Academic Evaluation.* San Francisco: Jossey-Bass, 1976.

A comprehensive volume anticipating the growing policy emphasis on accountability in the latter half of the 20th century. Furnishes an extensive guide to philosophy and method in the evaluation of student, program, faculty, and administrator performance. Offers informed commentary on institutional self-study and effectiveness and includes an extensive bibliography.

DuBois, W.E.B. *The Education of Black People: Ten Critiques, 1906-1960.* Edited by Herbert Aptheker, Amherst: University of Massachusetts Press, 1973.

Presents 10 major talks by this noted critic of racial segregation. DuBois discusses vocational education versus real "college" higher education for Negroes and the practices of several colleges for blacks, especially his alma mater, Fisk. Pleads eloquently for a better preparation of talented blacks for leadership roles in society.

D'Souza, Dinesh. *Illiberal Education: The Politics of Race and Sex on Campus.* New York: Free Press, 1991.

Relates in abundant detail the increasing politicization, admissions quotas, and the raw sensitivities of groups feeling victimized, which the author claims pervade many institutions at the century's end. A cause célèbre, the book provoked outrage from activists and drew praise for its exposure of some recent follies from academic traditionalists.

Eble, Kenneth. *The Craft of Teaching: A Guide to Mastering the Professor's Art.* San Francisco: Jossey-Bass, 1976. Second edition, 1988.

This lively little book argues that teaching at the college level is not work for an amateur and that teaching skills can be acquired and enhanced. Debunks a number of widely held myths about teaching and teacher effectiveness and explores a variety of instructional approaches designed to enrich teaching performance.

Eddy, Edward D., Jr. *Colleges for Our Land and Time: The Land-Grant Idea in American Education.* New York: Harper & Brothers, 1957.
An informative discussion of the development of land-grant colleges up to the 1950s. An analysis of the movement and its relationship to American society. Traces the conflicts in establishing A&M schools and the battles they have waged to shape and carry out their mission. A good beginning for continuing study.

Feldman, Kenneth, and Newcomb, Theodore. *The Impact of College on Students.* San Francisco: Jossey-Bass, 1969.
A pioneering work whose combination of thoughtfulness and breadth helped put higher education on the scholarly map as a legitimate, coherent field of study. Its forte is bringing social psychology as a lens into discussions of the college experience. This work synthesizes the original research of the authors and introduces readers to a prodigious body of secondary sources.

Flexner, Abraham. *Medical Education in the United States and Canada.* New York: Carnegie Foundation for Advancement of Teaching, 1910. Reprint, New York: Classics of Medicine Library, 1997.
This pioneering, investigative study of American medical education resulted in the closure of 20 medical schools before the report was released. Just before the turn of the 19th century, there were 160 medical schools in the United States; and at the conclusion of the Flexner study, that number had been reduced by nearly half. This study set the standard for other professional education fields by clearly placing medical education at post-baccalaureate level.

Flexner, Abraham. *Universities: English, German, American.* New York: Oxford University Press, 1930. Reprint, New Brunswick, N.J.: Transaction, 1994.
This critical analysis transposes the perspectives Flexner, always the scold, brought to bear on medical schools. The major source

of concern is the price paid for the university's popular appeal: losing its sense of clear purpose. But Flexner's critical vision coexisted with glaring blind spots. In praising the German university, Flexner glossed over the abuses of learning already taking root in German scholarship by the late 1920s.

Folger, John K.; Astin, Helen S.; and Bayer, Alan E. *Human Resources and Higher Education: Staff Report of the Commission on Human Resources and Advanced Education.* New York: Russell Sage Foundation, 1970.
A comprehensive but under-appreciated study of "how the nation identifies, educates, and utilizes men and women of high ability." Addresses demand and supply trends for arts and sciences graduates, factors that keep those trends in balance, career issues and trends for women and selected professions, the plans of high school and college students, and college graduate mobility.

Gaines, Thomas. *The Campus as a Work of Art.* New York: Praeger, 1991.
Develops the argument that thoughtfully designed spaces, rather than great individual buildings, are the essence of a memorable campus. Insists that one can find both good and bad campus design in any era. Profiles of selected institutions introduces readers to concepts of spatial design. Includes a good-natured list of the "Top 50" campuses.

Gardner, John W. *Excellence: Can We Be Equal and Excellent Too?* New York: Harper, 1961. Reprint, New York: Norton, 1984.
A small but widely read and cited volume on the encouragement of excellence in a democratic society and the delicate work of balancing equality of opportunity and excellence in performance expectation. Explores the philosophic tensions in a democratic society between competition and cooperation and stresses the varieties of excellence to be found and nurtured in diverse personalities.

Geiger, Roger. *To Advance Knowledge: The Growth of American Research Universities, 1900-1940.* New York: Oxford University Press, 1986.

A beautifully researched chronicle of how the top private and major state universities became powerful homes of research, especially in the sciences. Claims that the structure, forms of financing, and faculty interests were largely in place by 1920 and discusses how research increasingly came in conflict with older university obligations.

Goodman, Paul. *The Community of Scholars.* New York: Random House, 1962.

A major text of the 1960s, this book alleges that colleges and universities have grown too large and too dedicated to training professionals instead of educating young people for freedom and civic responsibility. A self-described "anarchist," the author suggests that institutions reduce administration drastically and break up into small communities of wide-ranging and liberating inquiry.

Grant, Gerald, and Riesman, David. *The Perpetual Dream: Reform and Experiment in American Education.* Chicago: University of Chicago Press, 1978.

Chronicles and analyzes the passion for reforming colleges in a thematic anthology of institutional profiles. The key organizing concept is "telic reform" — substantial, intentional innovation that counters the dominance and drift of the archetypal research university model. Grant and Riesman combine historical context with contemporary interviews to present a gallery of diverse colleges whose collective legacy is to show the varieties of reform and innovations charismatic leaders and their followers have embraced. The choice of profiles is compelling.

Harvard University Committee on the Objectives of General Education in a Free Society. *General Education in a Free Society.* Cambridge: Harvard University Press, 1945.

The best of several World War II-era reports on college education. Deals with general education at all levels. Explains education as a strong factor in the continuance of the liberal tradition essential to the preservation of civilization. Emphasizes that higher education is much more than the "mere acquisition of information for the development of special skills."

Haskins, Charles H. *The Rise of Universities.* New York: Henry Holt, 1923.
This slim volume is both enduring and endearing. Originally presented as lectures at Brown University, a prodigious body of scholarship on medieval universities is distilled to present a compact yet perceptive account of governance, curricula, and student life. Despite our contemporary glorification of gothic spires as a link with the medieval university, there was no "medieval university campus." The most significant legacy the medieval university has provided is the legal stature of the university as a chartered institution with the power to confer degrees.

Hawkins, Hugh. *Banding Together: The Rise of National Association in American Higher Education, 1887-1950.* Baltimore: Johns Hopkins University Press, 1923.
Discusses the origins of early efforts at interinstitutional cooperation in order to provide disparate higher education institutions and constituencies formal representation in Washington, D.C. For those familiar with the alphabet soup of ACE, AAU, AAHE, AASCU and NAICU, Hawkins' thorough research brings to life interesting alliances and negotiations. His work tempers tendencies to focus on the individual campus as the unit of analysis.

Henry, William, III. *In Defense of Elitism.* New York: Doubleday, 1994.
A crisp work offering a provocative and unflinching examination of the balance between egalitarian and elitist motives in American higher education. Examines the inclination for making curriculum and program decisions on a political basis, rather than

an educational basis, and explores issues being engaged in the academy: political correctness, feminism, affirmative action, multicultural curricula. Takes the position that the policy emphasis on egalitarianism and enhanced access to higher education in the latter half of the 20th century has produced much that is shallow and shoddy in academic programs and credentials.

Highet, Gilbert. *The Immortal Profession: The Joys of Teaching and Learning.* New York: Weybright and Talley, 1976.
A master teacher and classical scholar discusses teaching, its challenges and satisfactions, and gives remarkable insights into teacher-student relations affecting higher learning. His advice and opinions are firmly anchored in experience, erudition, and common sense.

Hodgkinson, Harold. *Institutions in Transition: A Profile of Change in Higher Education.* New York: McGraw-Hill, 1971.
Documents statistically the enormous changes that U.S. higher education went through in the 25 years following World War II, from the rise of mass higher education and community colleges to increased research and the sheer size of institutions. Includes five case studies to show how the changes occurred.

Hofstadter, Richard, and Metzger, Walter P. *The Development of Academic Freedom in the United States.* New York: Columbia University Press, 1955.
A well-focused consideration of the ideals and realities of academic freedom in colleges and universities — an undeniable classic in American higher education. Hofstadter's history of "the college" and Metzger's "the university" stand back-to-back as the best source of much that we know about academic practices in U.S. colleges and universities.

Hofstadter, Richard. *Anti-Intellectualism in American Life.* New York: Knopf, 1963.
Presents a combined thematic and chronological interpretation of the persistent tension between intellectuals and American socie-

ty. Its textures are subtle, because intellectualism has hardly been synonymous with or defined by academic structures. Fascination with the serious play of ideas, rather than degrees or rewards, is the crucial criterion for inclusion in the ranks of intellectuals. Time and time again academics are caught within and between worlds. Status as an expert, for example, provided both the opportunity for ideas to be influential and, at the same time, the lure to compress once original ideas into banal, albeit lucrative, formulae.

Horowitz, Helen L. *Campus Life: Undergraduate Cultures from the End of the Eighteenth Century to the Present.* New York: Knopf, 1987. Reprint, Chicago: University of Chicago Press, 1988.
Student subcultures are the conceptual focus for this well-written survey. Displeased with the aggressive ambition and intellectual apathy of undergraduates in the early 1980s, Horowitz unravels the riddle as to the way college life had always been. One message is a tendency for "college men" to dominate campuses with less than high regard for serious intellectual pursuits. "Rebels" and "outsiders" have leavened the campus composition and character. And such chapters as "Revenge of the Nerds" hint at the diversity and fluidity that can occur on the American campus.

Hutchins, Robert M. *The Higher Learning in America.* New Haven, Conn.: Yale University Press, 1936. Reprint, New Brunswick, N.J.: Transaction, 1995.
A work of modest length but not of modest impact. For Hutchins a community of scholars serves democracy best by being free to pursue intellectual interests without being confined or unfairly shaped by material or economic matters. Indeed, the two missions of pursuing truth for its own sake and preparing men and women for their life's work offer the university a dilemma of purposes. Hutchins is not bashful in suggesting that the vocational mission seriously infringes on the deeper and more important mission of the university as a center of independent thought.

Jacob, Philip. *Changing Values in College: An Exploratory Study
of the Impact of College Teaching.* New York: Harper & Row,
1957.
This was a disturbing research report when it was published.
Jacob claims that teaching in social studies and general education
has little long-term effect on students' beliefs and values. Only
the intellectual "climate" of some colleges was found to alter student values fundamentally.

Jaspers, Karl. *The Idea of the University.* Boston: Beacon Press,
1959.
An authority on philosophy, psychiatry, and existentialism, the
president of the University of Heidelberg offers his idea of the university: its implications for science and scholarship, technology
and the humanities, the university's relations with state and society. Dated but still profound.

Jencks, Christopher, and Riesman, David. *The Academic Revolution.* Garden City, N.Y.: Doubleday, 1968.
Places higher education as a subject onto the center stage. In a style
best described as historical sociology, the co-authors take the pulse
of higher education as part of the larger social and economic
changes in American life. An unexpected dimension of this study
was the attention it brought to the academic profession's rise to
power. By the time the book went to press, the unexpected prolif-
eration of campus protests gave the title an unintended association
with the imagined prospects of student revolution. The authors
depict an American society characterized by a "partial triumph of
meritocracy," with the actual gains in upward social mobility being
inflated by an overall rising tide of economic prosperity.

Keller, George. *Academic Strategy: The Management Revolution
in American Higher Education.* Baltimore: Johns Hopkins
University Press, 1983.
One of the more widely read and cited works on higher education
planning and management. Not altogether complimentary of the

past leadership, courage, and competence of some higher education presidents and academic leaders, this well-researched work
furnishes both an informative and conceptual basis for improving
college management and strategic planning. Considered by many
as the premier stimulus for the improvement of strategic planning
in American higher education.

Kennedy, Donald. *Academic Duty*. Cambridge: Harvard Univer-
    sity Press, 1997.
A principled guide to the seldom-explored subject of the obligations
of professors to their students, discipline, college or university, and
society. The author, a former president of Stanford, distributes wisdom and insight about contemporary faculty practices and implores
scholars to increase their loyalty to their home institutions and to
teaching.

Kerr, Clark. *The Uses of the University*. Cambridge, Mass.: Har-
    vard University Press, 1963. Fourth edition, 1995.
Kerr's memorably concise book is a classic. Kerr's several additions, postscripts, and prefaces over the years have allowed him
both to make and to write — and then re-write — the recent history of research universities. A brilliant and candid description of
what was happening to major institutions in the post-World War
II era.

Kerr, Clark, and Gade, Marion L. *The Many Lives of Academic
    Presidents: Time, Place, and Character*. Washington, D.C.: As-
    sociation of Governing Boards of Universities and Colleges,
    1986.
Insights from 800 interviews with college presidents, their spouses,
and other associates. Conveys a variety of presidential expectations and experiences and explores the different governance models and various roles presidents play as they make decisions in
changing contexts and environments.

Leslie, W. Bruce. *Gentlemen and Scholars: College and Community in the Age of the University, 1865 to 1917.* University Park: Pennsylvania State University Press, 1992.

To counter the conventional wisdom about the demise of the small college in the "age of the university," Leslie looks beyond the rhetoric of university advocates to examine the actual character and condition of colleges. Case studies of Bucknell, Princeton, Franklin and Marshall, and Swarthmore indicate that this institutional genre was healthy, respected, and diverse in the period 1865 to 1917. Includes data to suggest that faculty at many colleges lived well, were highly regarded, and even could afford to hire household servants.

Lipset, Seymour Martin. *Rebellion in the University.* Boston: Little, Brown, 1972. Reprint with new introduction by the author, New Brunswick, N.J.: Transaction, 1993.

An extraordinarily insightful, informed, and fair exploration of the student revolts of the 1960s and early 1970s. Includes a history of student activism and faculty political allegiances in America. The 26-page introduction to the 1993 edition contains an essay on recent student and faculty political actions.

Lucas, Christopher. *American Higher Education: A History.* New York: St. Martin's Press, 1994.

The mission of the American college and university to search for what is true, good, and beautiful has its roots in Greek antiquity. This well-written history unfolds like a good novel, furnishing a comprehensive examination of the principles of mission and operation that undergird the modern American college. It also provides a lively tour of the Greek, medieval, and early European heritage that enables readers to understand the conceptual foundations on which American higher education rests.

Marsden, George M. *The Soul of the American University: From Protestant Establishment to Established Non-Belief.* New York: Oxford University Press, 1994.

The early history of American higher education is a testimony to the driving force of religion in America. Why, then, would the contemporary home of intellect become less friendly to, or even disdain, the concerns of faith and religion, when matters of fact are so often driven by matters of faith? Marsden examines the lessening of religious influence and the rise of secularism. His work also offers an attractive narrative and critique of religion in American colleges and universities and explores the profound question of how truth is to be defined and discerned.

Mayhew, Lewis, and Ford, Patrick. *Reform in Graduate and Professional Education.* San Francisco: Jossey-Bass, 1974.
Depicts the increasing accent on field and clinical experiences and on behavioral sciences in professional education. The authors discuss such innovations in graduate education as admissions criteria, curricular flexibility, role of examinations, role of languages, quality assurance approaches, focus on interdisciplinary centers, and challenges of urban life. This thoughtful work anticipated most of the program and policy issues that remain under active scrutiny.

McConnell, Thomas R. *A General Pattern for American Public Higher Education.* New York: McGraw-Hill, 1962.
A senior statesman's clarion call for greater coordination of higher education with division of educational labor among colleges and universities to serve differing student needs amidst growing student diversity. Argues that the lack of coordination squanders human and financial resources and does not efficiently serve society's civic, cultural, and industrial needs.

Meiklejohn, Alexander. *The Experimental College.* New York: Harper, 1932.
Reports on the results of the author's first two years of college at the University of Wisconsin, where he combined study of ancient Greece and contemporary America. A poignant book by a noted

radical educator who argued that the main task of a university is to teach people to think clearly and deeply and to deal with the big issues.

Millett, John D. *The Academic Community: An Essay on Organization.* New York: McGraw-Hill, 1962.
This easy-to-read volume makes clear the difference in organizational culture and structure between college organizations and corporate organizations. Explores the marriage of hierarchy/ bureaucratic principles with collegial/consensus principles in the orchestration of power interactions among faculty, students, administration, and alumni. This pattern of multiple stakeholders and shared authority is featured as yet another distinction in college and university governance and community. Contends that conflict in academic organizations is not necessarily an enemy of community.

Millett, John D. *Conflict in Higher Education.* San Francisco: Jossey-Bass, 1984.
An instructive work on the emerging role of state governments' voice in the governance of American higher education. Explores the tension that developed between the campus desire for autonomy and state interest in accountability. Describes the forms and degree of state regulation of campuses; reveals conflicts between campus and state on issues of mission distinction, resource allocation, and quality assurance; and stresses the partnership values of understanding, patience, and civility for both academic and political leaders.

Mortimer, Kenneth, and McConnell, T.R. *Sharing Authority Effectively.* San Francisco: Jossey-Bass, 1978.
Offers both a descriptive and critical analysis of the culture of shared authority and decision making for colleges and universities, in which the roles and interests of internal constituents — faculty, administrators, students, trustees — intersect with those of external stakeholders, such as coordinating boards, executive and legislative bodies, and courts. Explores the tension between

formal and functional authority: Who has the right to make decisions and who has the competence to make decisions? Includes
an examination of collective bargaining in higher education governance and nicely outlines the efficiency, quality, and accountability concerns that have increased governance complexity of
American higher education in the latter half of the 20th century.

Newman, Frank. *Choosing Quality: Reducing Conflict Between
the State and the University.* Denver: Education Commission
of the States, 1978.
A concise volume that details the sources of conflict between
campus and state, exploring differences in perspective, interests,
and goals but also pointing to issues of integrity and quality that
invite increased oversight, regulation, and intrusion of the state
into campus management. Also stresses the importance of civic
aspiration and political will at the state level in building campuses
and state systems of high quality and emphasizes shared responsibility.

Olson, Keith. *The G.I. Bill, the Veterans, and the Colleges.* Lex-
ington: University Press of Kentucky, 1974.
Tersely describes the origins and effects of one of the nation's
most inventive social programs of the past half-century. A revealing text about a bold benefit for war veterans, one that helped
change U.S. higher education.

Ortega y Gasset, Jose. *Mission of the University.* Princeton:
Princeton University Press, 1944.
Lectures at the University of Madrid in the 1930s, outlining four
missions of the university: to train for the learned professions,
political leadership, research, and to develop through general
education cultured individuals who understand their surround-
ings and are conversant in the great themes and ideas of the day.

Pace, C. Robert. *Measuring Outcomes of College: Fifty Years of
Findings and Recommendations for the Future.* San Francisco:
Jossey-Bass, 1979.

A quantitative survey of higher education, synthesizing data from several major studies from the 1930s to the 1970s. Discusses student achievement in college, the relationship between college and postgraduate attitudes and experiences, and other measures of achievement and accomplishment.

Pascarella, Ernest T., and Terenzini, Patrick T. *How College Affects Students: Findings and Insights from Twenty Years of Research.* San Francisco: Jossey-Bass, 1991.
A comprehensive and eye-opening meta-evaluation of some 2,600 research studies detailing the effect of college on student cognitive growth, values and attitudes, psychosocial changes, career attainment, moral development, and economic benefits. Features summary tables and exploration of effect by college type and size. Finds that what a college does with students is more important than where students attend college, that student-faculty interaction makes a big difference, and many other revealing insights.

Pelikan, Jaroslav. *The Idea of the University. A Reexamination.* New Haven, Conn.: Yale University Press, 1992.
A fascinating discussion of Cardinal Newman's "Idea" with equally interesting views of Pelikan's own definition of "the university." As Newman's intellectual equal, Pelikan provides perspectives and insights that are unlikely to be found elsewhere. A classic interpretation of "the classic" on universities by a noted historian of Western ideas.

President's Commission on Higher Education. *Higher Education for American Democracy: A Report of the President's Commission on Higher Education.* New York: Harper, 1948.
A six-volume report by a panel chaired by George Zook, this project looked at increasing access to formal education beyond high school. It was the complement to Vannevar Bush's successful case for continuing federal research funding of "big science" as a permanent part of national policies. The "Truman Commis-

sion Report" provided a blueprint of sorts for federal policies toward higher education for the post-World War II era but was limited in its impact because it was not tied to any federal legislation or funding. Nonetheless, it did present an early warning about demographic changes and voiced ideas ranging from expanded college enrollments to goals of racial integration and equity. Its discussion of educational opportunity presaged the issues of "separate but equal" that surfaced six years later in *Brown v. Board of Education*. In matters of affordability, the commission report kindled serious consideration of policies on low tuition or massive student financial aid.

Rourke, Francis, and Brooks, Glenn. *The Managerial Revolution in Higher Education.* Baltimore: Johns Hopkins Press, 1966.
One of the earliest policy research volumes reflecting the transformation from management by tradition and feeling to management by fact, from seat-of-the-pants approaches to the application of information intelligence and analysis in policy making, decision making, and planning. The volume describes the growing role of the computer as a powerful information tool, features the emergence of institutional research, and describes the move from the "solitary splendor" of college administrators to styles of management marked by openness and candor and the sharing of information for decision making.

Rudolph, Frederick. *The American College and University: A History.* New York: Vintage Books, 1962. Reprint with new introduction and supplemental bibliography by John Thelin, Athens: University of Georgia Press, 1990.
Stands out as a classic survey and interpretation of American colleges and universities. Witty, lively, and well-written, it also has become a favorite target of a new generation of critics. Rudolph readily acknowledged that his work was limited in its focus on the four-year institutions, what we now call the "traditional campus." Distinctive contributions include the historical significance of students as characters in the higher education drama. Dis-

cusses at length the extracurriculum, ranging from literary soci-
eties to intercollegiate sports.

Ruml, Beardsley. *Memo to a College Trustee.* New York: McGraw-
    Hill, 1959.
Proposes controversial cost-cutting measures to help colleges run
more efficiently. Raises questions about how institutions are
organized and inefficiencies of curriculum, class size, and teaching arrangements. Proposes "models of the possible." Suggests
that trustees take a more active role in managing escalating education costs.

Sanford, Nevitt, ed. *The American College: A Psychological and
    Social Interpretation of the Higher Learning.* New York: John
    Wiley and Sons, 1962.
Regarded in the 1960s as *the* book on higher education, the
essays in this widely varied study run the gamut of students and
professors, teaching and learning, campus life and culture, college environments and effects, and the social-psychological contexts of higher learning. A bold attempt to appraise U.S. colleges
in their entirety.

Schmidt, G.P. *The Old Time College President.* Columbia Univer-
    sity Studies in History, Economics, and Public Law, no. 317.
    New York: Columbia University Press, 1930.
An informative and interesting discussion of college presidents
between 1760 and 1860. Evaluates the college presidency and
considers the various roles the early presidents were called on to
play: religious leader, patriot, administrator, teacher, reformer,
admissions recruiter, fundraiser, and reactionary. Insightful and
interesting.

Slosson, Edwin E. *Great American Universities.* New York:
    Macmillan, 1910. Reprint, New York: Ayer, 1977.
A highly informative volume — and required reading — for anyone interested in the history of American universities. Written by

a journalist with a Ph.D., this is the best introduction to higher education in the early years of the 20th century. Comprehensive, fact-filled, and well-written.

Smith, Huston. *The Purposes of Higher Education.* New York: Harper, 1955. Reprint, Westwood, Conn.: Greenwood, 1971.
An expansion of a committee report from Washington University on liberal education, this work explores six philosophical value dichotomies (for example, relativism-objectivity, freedom-authority). From this analysis emerge 19 well-articulated aims of a liberal education. A searching philosophical analysis of the bases of a college education.

Snow, C.P. *The Two Cultures and the Scientific Revolution.* New York: Cambridge University Press, 1959.
A provocative little book that argues that modern science and technology have created a revolution in thought and action and that knowledge and the techniques of both are scarcely comprehended by the other campus culture of literary, artistic, and social studies. Contends that we need to redesign higher education to reduce the chasm between the two realms of intellect.

Solomon, Barbara. *In the Company of Educated Women: A History of Women and Higher Education in America.* New Haven, Conn.: Yale University Press, 1985.
A well-researched history on the demands by women for increased education access, career choice, and civic voice and on the opposition they encountered in advancing the rights and opportunities of women in higher education and society. Narrates how the women's movement and feminism enriched curriculum development and campus life but does not neglect debates among women themselves on these issues.

Solomon, Lewis, and Taubman, Paul. *Does College Matter? Some Evidence on the Impact of Higher Education.* New York: Academic Press, 1973.

A collection of essays featuring research studies, literature searches, and reflective overviews by leading scholars and policy researchers. Touches on topics from a definition of college quality, rationale for federal support of higher education, and measurement of college outputs to perspectives on the role and contribution of historically black colleges. Suggests that college does indeed matter in areas such as change in personality, income potential, values, motivation, and self-efficacy and that college is a major contributor to the development of "human capital." Also touches on the disproportionate economic benefit to whites as compared to blacks at this time in higher education history.

Spectorsky, Auguste C., ed. *The College Years.* New York: Hawthorn Books, 1958.
Spectorsky, long famous and respected as editor of *Esquire* magazine, carefully gathered and edited a fascinating anthology of fiction, memoirs, poetry, photographs, and essays about college life from the medieval period into the post-World War II era. Its first effect is to remind casual readers how special colleges and the campus experience have been. On closer reading, one finds out in detail *why* this institution has been both memorable and varied in its influence on students, faculty, alumni, and the larger public.

Sperber, Murray. *College Sports, Inc.: The Athletic Department vs. the University.* New York: Henry Holt, 1990.
Murray Sperber's insightful tour through American intercollegiate athletic departments dispels any wishful thinking that college sports are truly a student activity. His major point is that at NCAA Division I institutions, the intercollegiate athletic department is a legally separate, incorporated entity that is propped up by privileges and is exempt from virtually all accountability and compliance requirements faced by academic units. Sperber dispels erroneous notions — namely, that big-time college sports "make a lot of money." Not for the faint-hearted.

Spurr, Stephen. *Academic Degree Structures: Innovative Approaches.* New York: McGraw-Hill, 1970.
One of several influential research and policy volumes issued by the Carnegie Commission on Higher Education. This volume traces the history of academic credentials, presents a theory of degree structures, and chronicles the considerable expansion in degree titles at every degree level (associate, bachelor, master, doctoral) in American colleges and universities. Includes a particularly informative chapter on the increase in type and number of degrees in the professions and creative arts.

Storr, Richard. *The Beginnings of Graduate Education in America.* Chicago: University of Chicago Press, 1953.
Succinctly traces the origins and early attempts to establish graduate education and research activities in higher education prior to the Civil War. Reveals that major changes in higher education often have long gestation periods and require many proponents.

Thelin, John. *Games Colleges Play: Scandal and Reform in Intercollegiate Athletics.* Baltimore: Johns Hopkins University Press, 1994.
A well-researched analysis of the distinctive relationship between academics and athletics in American higher education — a strained connection that, no matter one's attitudes toward the role of athletics, has been central to the life of American colleges and universities for more than a century. Offers an engaging historical panorama, moving from such earlier studies as the 1929 Savage study of American intercollegiate athletics, which centered on the increased commercialism of sport, to the 1991 Knight reform report. This book builds on a close investigation of institutional records, archives, and public documents. A rich documentary for anyone who wants to understand the complexity surrounding athletics and academics in higher education.

Thwing, Charles Franklin. *The College President.* New York: Macmillan, 1926.

An intriguing perspective on the college presidency. Describes the internal and external relationships a president must nourish. Discusses the qualities and characteristics a president must exhibit and develop — both as an individual and as a professional. Considers the various perils and rewards of the presidency and their implications for effective leadership.

Trueblood, Elton. *The Idea of a College.* New York: Harper, 1959. This proposal for an ideal college addresses teachers, students, administrators, the curriculum, and issues in coeducation and the relationship between the college and society. A good primer for many later volumes about the ingredients of a superior college.

Turner, Paul Venable. *Campus: An American Planning Tradition.* New York: Architectural History Foundation, 1984. Describes, with numerous illustrations and informed prose, the architectural history of U.S. college and university campuses. Notes that the American academic campus is a distinctive contribution to world architecture and community design.

Van Doren, Mark. *Liberal Education.* New York: Holt, 1943. Written during World War II, this book advocates increased liberal education in colleges following the war. Lays out the contents of a good education and a good curriculum and gently suggests the study of the finest books and the newest science and technology. Contains a rich number of aphorisms and keen observations about learning and life.

Veblen, Thorstein. *The Higher Learning in America: A Memorandum on the Conduct of Universities by Business Men.* New York: B.W. Huebsch, 1918. Veblen used his training as an anthropologist and economist, fused with biting sarcasm, to scrutinize American college governance. Demonstrates to readers why he had the dubious claim of having been both hired and fired by many great universities. The analyst who contributed such familiar terms as "the leisure class" used this work to identify and dissect the "Captains of Erudition" — industrialists and businessmen who had gained a stronghold on American college and university boards of trustees.

Veysey, Laurence. *The Emergence of the American University.*
  Chicago: University of Chicago Press, 1965.
This book is an exemplar of scholarship transformed, a brilliant dissertation that became an important book. Veysey's work furnishes an historical account of the philosophical contentions that shaped the modern American university. Veysey reminds us of the philosophical conflicts over mission and governance, over curriculum and campus life issues that have characterized academic dialogue. Offering more than an insight into issues of goal and command in academic life, it also offers insight into the lives and thoughts of those education statesmen who created and sustained constructive policy conversation beyond the environs of their universities.

Whitehead, Alfred N. *The Aims of Education and Other Essays.*
  New York: Macmillan, 1929.
No one has written so penetratingly or wisely as philosopher Whitehead about the purposes and tasks of higher education — and the dangers of pedantry. A brilliant set of essays by a stylist who wrote lines such as, "Knowledge does not keep any better than fish." Worth reading annually.

Wilson, Logan. *The Academic Man: A Study in the Sociology of a Profession.* London: Oxford University Press, 1942. Reprint, Brunswick, N.J.: Transaction, 1995. *American Academic: Then and Now.* New York: Oxford University Press, 1964.
A good introduction to academic professions, their unique environment, and the ways colleges and universities function. The first volume was written as a young sociologist; the second from the Olympian perspective of a former president of the University of Texas and the American Council on Education.

Wolff, Robert Paul. *The Ideal of the University.* Boston: Beacon
  Press, 1969. Reprint, New Brunswick, N.J.: Transaction, 1992.
Analyzes the kinds of institutions within modern higher education, suggests "partisan thoughts" and "utopian reforms," and
proposes new forms of campus governance. Contains striking
ideas by a gifted, idealistic radical.

Wolfle, Dael. *America's Resources of Specialized Talent: A Current Appraisal and a Look Ahead.* New York: Harper, 1954.
A highly constructive critique of the world of education, employ-
ment, the discovery and development of human talents, and the
greatly diversified careers of college graduates in post-World War
II society and economy. Argues forcefully for the nourishing of
America's most talented persons.

The Changing World of Books About Higher Education

by Cameron Fincher

> Some books are to be tasted, others to be swallowed, and
> some few to be chewed and digested.
> —Francis Bacon, *On Studies*

Since entering college in 1946, I have read or heard Bacon's quote many times. Books have always played an important role in my life, and I have never doubted the wisdom of his advice.

In 1964, however, when my professorial career path changed direction and required moving to the University of Georgia in Athens, my entire professional library in higher education consisted of only four volumes. Along with several hundred psychology and history volumes, I packed Hofstadter and Metzger's *Development of Academic Freedom*, Sanford's edited volume on *The American College*, Brubacher and Rudy's *Higher Education in Transition*, and Caplow and McGee's *Academic Marketplace*. For the next 34 years these four volumes could be quickly retrieved from a bookshelf immediately behind my desk chair. Each book was consulted frequently, referenced or reread, and recommended to others. Through my work in the Institute of Higher Education, I acquired numerous other fine books about higher education, some of which I merely tasted but many that I chewed and digested.

The credibility of our list of 100 classic books can be said to rest firmly on our experiences as avid readers of the published literature in higher education and the process we have gone through in sifting and sorting, faxing and phoning, reviewing and annotating books that we hope will be read by others interested in higher education. I would like to think that every book on our list will be interesting to readers and will make an appreciable return on the readers' investment of time and effort.

My personal delight in working with the co-authors on this work stems, no doubt, from my continuing efforts in the development of higher education as a field of doctoral study and my increasing concern with what I believe to be the cloudy climate of scholarship in the later years of the 20th century. I hope that future curricula in American higher education need not be improvised as much as courses and programs have been in the past.

In 1968, when the University of Georgia's Institute of Higher Education was asked to develop a doctoral program in higher education, most of the books on our list had not been published, and suitable textbooks were difficult to find. Fortunately, we met the many curricular needs by using the commission reports then appearing almost monthly. The Carnegie Commission on Higher Education, established in 1967, issued during its five years of productivity a large number of technical reports, critical essays, commissioned studies, and reports with policy recommendations.

Other timely and relevant reports were issued by the Assembly on University Goals and Governance, the HEW Task Force on Higher Education, and the Commission on Human Resources and Advanced Education (whose report was authored by John Folger, Helen Astin, and Alan Bayer and is included in our list of classics). Equally important and indicative of the Carnegie Commission's influence was the Educational Amendments Act of 1972. If the curricula of higher education were sometimes lacking in substance, national commissions and task forces were not to blame. The 1970s proved to be an especially seminal decade for the study of colleges and universities.

In 1973 an issue of *Journal of Research and Development in Education (JRDE)* was dedicated to higher education as "an emerging discipline" in the midst of a national "need for reform." In the lead article, Collins Burnett[1] found the professional literature of higher education to be quite promising. Because many professors of higher education in those early years were apostates from other disciplines, a substantial portion of the publications in higher education consisted of what the behavioral and social sciences had to say about colleges and universities. As editor of the issue, I believed that the behavioral and social sciences could provide the interdisciplinary approach needed in higher education programs, and so I contributed an article with that emphasis.[2]

Indeed, the promising future of the behavioral sciences was one of the premises on which centers and institutes of higher education had been organized. The Center for the Study of Higher Education at Berkeley, the Center for the Study of Higher Education at Michigan, and the Institute of Higher Education at Columbia were producing the research doctoral programs needed in higher education, and the Institute of Higher Education in Georgia was defining its mission as an interdisciplinary effort in instruction, research, and service.

As noted by Collins Burnett, at least 36 professional journals were receptive to articles dealing with the study of colleges and universities, and the ERIC Clearinghouse on Higher Education could report the availability of more than 1,330 recently acquired documents pertaining to higher education. Also available by 1973 were two compiled bibliographies: one dealing with "The Community Junior College" and the other with "The Learning Climate in the Liberal Arts College." However, contributors to the *JRDE* issue cited far more journal articles, conference proceedings, foundation reports, and edited volumes than substantive books written by recognized scholars and distributed by reputable publishers. Thus in 1973 a distinctive body of professional literature was in the making but not yet available in books deal-

---

[1]Collins W. Burnett, "Higher Education as a Specialized Field of Study," *Journal of Research and Development in Education* 6, no. 2 (1973): 4-15.
[2]"The Behavioral Sciences as an Interdisciplinary Approach," pp. 80-92.

ing specifically with higher education as an academic discipline or professional specialty.

What Does 100 Classic Books Tell Us?

Throughout the months in which George Keller, Grady Bogue, John Thelin, and I were discussing the selection and annotation of books representing higher education, I wondered how our list of 100 classics could be of assistance to colleagues who teach courses and direct doctoral research in higher education. We know, of course, that there are numerous college and university trustees, presidents, vice presidents, deans, directors, department heads, government officials, and state legislators who also can benefit from a better knowledge of higher education in general.

Of course, I was interested in how well the substance and contents of 100 books could reflect the expansion and development of collegiate and university education over the past 100 years. And I was interested in the continuing emergence of higher education as specialized or graduate education and in the quality of scholarly research within an academic discipline actively studying institutions of higher learning. To some extent, every book is indicative of its time and place — and each volume annotated in this book offers perspectives and insights that are historical, comparative, or developmental. At the same time, each book contains glimpses, hints, or nuances pertaining to past events, movements, and trends that some writer believed worthy of recording for someone's reading pleasure or benefit.

Perspectives and Insights

The historical development of the nation's colleges and universities, their programs and services, and their constituencies is reflected in the books chosen for annotation. Almost one in four books could be classified as history of one kind or another, and at least one in five books could be regarded as dealing with academic administration, presidential leadership, or policy issues. At least 18 books focus on institutional missions, goals, or objectives; and at least 11 books address curricular issues while another 11 books consider faculty responsibilities or teaching. Seven books are related to students or access and equity issues. Two books each discuss: technology, campus design, college life, athletics — and one, the community colleges.

The historical, comparative, and developmental perspectives reflected in these books verify a conclusion drawn many years prior to their selection. That is, to comprehend and appreciate American institutions of higher education, it is necessary to study their historical development at comparative stages of growth and maturation. As Columbia's John Herman Randall Jr. once wrote:

> To understand any belief, any ideal, any custom, any institution, we must examine its gradual growth from primitive beginnings to its present form. . . . Time and history are of fundamental importance.[3]

To this end, those who would understand the growth of American universities would be well-advised to read Veyzey's *Emergence of the American University,* followed by Slosson's *Great American Universities.* Continue on to Geiger's *To Advance Knowledge: The Growth of American Research Universities, 1900-1940,* and then follow the trail throughout the post-World War II era and into the 1990s. In much the same manner, benefits can be gained from reading together the two books on college faculty by Logan Wilson. One was written as a young sociologist in the 1930s and published in 1942. The other, published in 1964, was written as the former president of the University of Texas and then-president of the American Council on Education. John Corson provides before and after portraits of academic governance in 1960 and in 1975, while John Millet discusses the academic community prior to the 1960s and the later conflicts between institutional autonomy and public demands for accountability in the 1980s. Alexander Astin's revision in 1993 of his

---

[3]John Herman Randall Jr., *Making of the Modern Mind: A Survey of the Intellectual Background of the Present Age*, Fifth Anniversary Edition, with a foreword by Jacques Barzun (New York: Columbia University Press, 1976).

1977 book provides insight into the changing beliefs, attitudes, and knowledge of students. With respect to time and place, nine books on our list were published prior to the 1932 election of Franklin Delano Roosevelt to the U.S. presidency, and seven books were published during the Depression and war years of 1937-48. But slightly more than half (53 of the 100) were published between 1948 and 1980, the years of cold war, rapid college growth, student protests, and funding gains and setbacks. In the 1980s, 18 of the chosen books were published, and 13 other books were issued in the 1990s and recognized as books worthy of inclusion on the list. The study of higher education is clearly a growth field.

It is interesting to note the diversity of publishers issuing outstanding books in higher education between 1910 and 1997. Commercial publishers were the major producers (65 volumes), with university presses following with 28 volumes. Until Jossey-Bass took the lead with 18 volumes, the major publishers were Harper and Brothers (later Harper & Row, then HarperCollins) with 11 volumes, McGraw-Hill with eight volumes, and Oxford University Press with five. Holt and Macmillan each published three. The university presses issuing first editions of the books were Johns Hopkins (four volumes), followed by Yale and Chicago, each publishing three. The other first-edition publishers included foundations, the federal government, and seven other commercial publishers. Twenty-one of the 100 classics have been reprinted by various publishers, with Jossey-Bass (four) and Transaction Publishers (six) leading the way.

Authors and Academic Disciplines

Turning to the authors of books in higher education, we can appreciate the continuing influence of scholars and researchers in related fields of study. No single academic discipline or professional specialty can claim exclusive rights to scholarship in either higher education in general or as an "emerging" discipline. Among the authors are 11 historians and 11 sociologists, but there also are 10 authors closely identified with education research and scholarly inquiry.

Our indebtedness to the behavioral and social sciences would be quite evident if the 11 authors identified with sociology are combined with seven authors schooled in political science, five in economics, and six in psychology — a total of 29 authors. Contributions from the humanities must be acknowledged with four volumes by authors identified with philosophy, three with literature, and at least five of the nine authors who served as college or university presidents. In addition, recognition should be given to seven or eight authors whose total publications eclipse their contributions to higher education *per se.* Indeed, the visibility of so many authors in other fields of scholarly inquiry is an added benefit in the emergence of higher education as a multidisciplinary field of doctoral study — and as an increasingly valuable component of higher education's relevance in the nation's economic, technological, and cultural advancement.

The careers of no less than 18 authors would be regarded as illustrious by any measure, and their contributions to national thought and discussion are one reason why higher education has become a valuable *and* renewable national resource. Although Nevitt Sanford's pioneering 1961 book, *The American College,* has been referred to as a "foray into an undeveloped field" by social psychologists, all students of higher education should be grateful for the numerous benefits that are still evident. Indeed, Sanford's volume may be as good a place as any to begin one's study of the nation's colleges and universities. Among Sanford's "raiders" were many who stayed to cultivate the new ground and to establish higher education as an academic discipline.

Also among the illustrious names are Jaspers, Ortega, and Whitehead, best known for their books on philosophy; and Barzun, Highet, and Van Doren, well known for their scholarly books in other fields. On most university campuses, the names of Abraham Flexner, Daniel Bell, William Buckley, James G. March, and C.P. Snow can be used without being greeted with blank stares. John Gardner may be mentioned as the author of two books, *Excellence* (on our list) and *Self-Renewal,* that issued national, institutional, and individual challenges to readers. And the noted historian,

Richard Hofstadter, will be mentioned, sooner or later, in any informed discussion of the history of higher education.

Within the academic ranks of higher education the names of Cowley, McConnell, Millett, Bowen, Dressel, and Mayhew will be recognized as belonging to the "founding fathers" of higher education as a discipline. Clark Kerr will be recognized as the nation's most famous university ex-president and as the "visible hand" behind the numerous reports and recommendations issued by the Carnegie Commission on Higher Education and the Carnegie Council on Policy Studies. He also will be recognized as the co-author (with Marion Gade) of the most informative book yet written on the academic presidency in the United States. And although listed as "co-author" on only two books included on our list, the name of David Riesman will be recognized in virtually all corners of university campuses.

Moving closer to the programs and services of American colleges and universities, the names of Astin, Cross, Clark, Eddy, Jacobs, and Pace will be recognized for the books they have written on learning and teaching, admissions, examinations and grading, and retaining and graduating students. Their books have influenced numerous others who have accepted the challenge of writing their own books and journal articles. Astin is probably the most frequently cited author identified with higher education; and with his wife, Helen, as co-author of a volume (also with Folger and Bayer), the Astins are the only husband and wife authors to be found on our list.

Given the recognizability of many of these authors, it may be advisable to disclaim author name recognition as either a determinant or condition of a book's inclusion in our selection. To the contrary, all four authors of this book agreed that substance and content were far more important than categorical judgment or representativeness. No books are included as the best example of this or that kind of writing, this or that point of view, or typical of this or that trend, movement, or development in the field of higher education. In fact, to a remarkable extent, there were no prolonged or agonizing arguments on whether this or that kind of book should be included or excluded. If biased at all in our selections — which we were, of course — we would like to think that each choice was biased only by the book's quality and historical importance and by its appeal to our intellectual interests and experience. In our efforts to include books on their own merits, the four of us were well aware that it was much more difficult to remove books from the final list than to add them.

In brief, inclusion in the initial list required only a good case made by one of us to at least one other — or two votes cast in favor of inclusion. Deletion, however, required discussion and gentle persuasion by at least one of us, who could make a better case for a book's absence than its presence. If we were idealistic in our initial recommendation of books for inclusion, we became quite realistic in pruning the list to an even 100 books.

Themes, Trends, and Issues

In looking over the final list I am convinced that we do no disservice to anyone in calling the 100 books "classics" in higher education. Although I am amazed at the many different topics and issues included, I wonder about the extent to which the 100 books reflect a distinctive body of professional literature and how comprehensive their coverage might be. I also wonder what our collective choices tell us about the development of higher education as an academic discipline or field of doctoral study in American universities. A perusal of the list suggests that these 100 books deal with an increasingly large segment of the education enterprise during a period when science, technology, and education were obviously among the most prominent contributors to our nation and society and Western culture writ large.

A majority of the books have been written with a historical perspective. In 1910 Slosson's *Great American Universities* pointed to institutions that were a recent addition to the nation's cultural landscape. Veysey's book (1965) tells how these universities emerged from earlier arrays of Colonial, church-related, and state-chartered colleges. Other books (for example, Hawkins,

Thwing, Haskins, Schmidt, and Veblen) tell us about internal and environmental difficulties. Later authors (Geiger, Hutchins, Olsen, and Hofstadter) tell us fascinating stories about mid-century growth and maturation. And the numerous authors writing in the 1960s through the 1980s tell us about three incredible decades of expansion and accomplishments. Authors writing in the 1990s continue the analyses and interpretations of earlier years and call attention to our continuing need for reform and renewal.

From the developmental perspective of authors, we gain a better appreciation of the professors, instructors, students, graduates, and other university constituents as they deal with public needs, perceptions, and expectations in a rapidly changing climate. And from the comparative perspective we gain an even better historical perspective, by appreciating how much our institutions of higher learning, their purposes and functions, and their programs and services have changed. And they continue to change in a multinational economy driven by technological innovation in a shrinking global environment.

None of the outstanding books listed here will likely be found on other lists of the best books written during the 20th century. Although none of the books are sagas, dramas, or epics, each tells its own story of time and place. Taken as a whole, or taken one at a time by careful sampling, the books make a commendable contribution to our understanding of higher education over the course of the last century. Running through the various themes and topics of the books is the continuing development of higher education as an intellectual, utilitarian, sociocultural institution that still has much to learn about itself. Despite the overly publicized constancy of change, there is a remarkable continuity. And within its many traditions, conventions, and even its pedantic foolishness, there is an appreciable receptivity to the kind of change that was once regarded as "progress."

Granting all the faults that others may find, the books annotated in this volume do identify a significant body of literature that should be appreciated by the pluralistic constituencies of

American colleges and universities. With all the misinformation that can result from a hastily read annotation of a book — and despite the tendency of immature students to draw superficial conclusions from skimmed annotations of books they will never read — there are many occasions on which a careful reading of an annotation can supply an initial grasp of a book's contents and stimulate additional thinking, if not further reading.

In addition to identifying a body of literature, a list of books with annotations may be one of the better ways to define an academic discipline or field of advanced study. Even in the best colleges of education there can be an absence of perspective and insight concerning the administration, governance, funding, performance, and productivity of the university as an institution. On every enlightened college or university campus there will be quiet corners in which professors conduct experiments, write books, or teach classes with little awareness of the public policy issues affecting their institution and its future.

In closing, it is well to re-emphasize the intrinsic merits of books in institutions of higher learning. Should anyone ask, "Why books and not journals, magazines, and other periodicals?" the best answer might be, "Because books are more likely to contain and convey the best that has been thought, discussed, and written in our western intellectual tradition." Journal articles and other publications have their own merits in scientific, scholarly, and leisurely inquiry; and other communications media give brilliant promise of their own millennium of access to data, information, and knowledge. But as xerography has proved so quietly, none of us gains knowledge or wisdom by the mere possession of journal articles, reprints, or books. To learn, most of us must read, observe, think, discuss, and reflect. And for the immediate future, books will continue to be a truly remarkable means of learning about the things that matter most.

A brilliant but cynical scholar once said that any assistant professor could deliver a lecture on the university's purposes and functions — but no other faculty member would willingly attend such a lecture. Neither brilliance nor cynicism could have condoned the same statement about professors who write and publish a book on the university's purposes, programs, and services — and the many advantages or benefits of higher learning.

Let me conclude by returning to the quote with which I began. Two sentences later, Francis Bacon wrote:

> Reading maketh a full man; conference a ready man; and writing an exact man. And therefore, if a man write little he had need for a great memory; if he confer little, he had need have a present wit; and if he read little, he had need much cunning, to seem to know that he doth not.

Let the reader substitute the word *scholar* wherever Bacon used the word *man*; then, let the reader agree or disagree with Bacon. Either way, the reader will learn something from a book written long ago.

Searching for the Soul
of American
Higher Education

by E. Grady Bogue

One of the more obvious themes to emerge from our list of 100 of the 20th century's most notable books on American higher education is the transformation in mission expectations for our colleges and universities. The search for the soul of American higher education, its *raison d'etre* and philosophical essence, and the record of intellectual and political conflicts accompanying that search, can be found in many of our classic books. In *The Soul of the American University,* for example, George Marsden directed our attention to a transformation in mission from instruction in religion, the study of moral philosophy, and a belief in God toward a mission of science, pragmatism, and relativism. He poses this question, for example, on the mission issue of whether science and faith can coexist:

> In a world where there were no longer self-evident first principles based on God-created natural laws, what happened when allegedly scientific definitions of the "good" conflicted? How could one argue, for instance, that all humans are "created equal" if one denied that humans were created? (p. 375)

I find it paradoxical to frame an essay about searching for the soul of American higher education while acknowledging that some colleagues might believe that the concept of soul has no meaning. And how paradoxical can it be to acknowledge that the argument over the existence or nonexistence of a soul is a part of the essence of American higher education?

Indeed, there are American scholars who would contend that the maintenance of argument, the continuing contention of ideas, is fundamental not only to the spirit of American higher education but to the health of American democracy. In a core sense, then, American higher education may be seen as an organized argument, and this may be one of its most important contributions to a democratic society. Ideological contention is a "soul" condition. In *The Higher Learning in America* (1936) Robert Hutchins called attention to the mission conflict of whether liberal education should coexist with professional and vocational education:

> Vocationalism leads, then, to triviality and isolation; it debases the course of study and the staff; it deprives the university of its only excuse for existence, which is to provide a haven where the search for truth may go on unhampered by utility or pressure for "results." (p. 43)

If the development of American higher education had followed Hutchins, perhaps we would not have great professional and other "applied" schools associated with the American university. Nor would we have birthed extensive continuing education programs, which surely must be counted among the most dramatic mission additions of the late 20th century. In contrast, Clark Kerr celebrated the complexity of the "multiversity." In *The Uses of the University,* Kerr described the American university of the last century as an intellectual city of many communities, marked the distinctive American development of the public service mission, and highlighted the growing interaction of the "knowledge industry" with corporations and government.

In the 20th century, ideas and well-equipped minds became important resources, as important perhaps as land and natural resources; and trained intelligence became indispensable for America's economic and military welfare. Thus the call for higher education to serve economic development goals and to respond to

marketplace principles is one of the more obvious mission trans-
formations in the 20th century. Indeed, the pressure of marketplace
concepts on higher education governance, curriculum, finance,
and accountability marks another tension in the search for the
soul of American higher education. Will market pressures confine
and distort the search for truth in the distinctive culture of
American colleges and universities? Will college faculty become
hired hands and eager entrepreneurs, rather than custodians of
truth? Will college presidents become captains of enterprise,
rather than erudition? Will the house of intellect become a house
of merchandise where faculty are salesmen hawking their intellectual wares to students as credential hungry customers? This is
precisely what Thorstein Veblen feared in his 1918 book, *The
Higher Learning in America.*

In American democratic society, profit is a human motivator
and an engine of notable power. This is one real world. But service also is a human motivator and an important constructive force.
This also is a real world. In a democratic society, these two
motives are essential and complementary. Honest sweat may fall
from the brow of both industrialists and dreamers. Practical men
and women may march to the power of ideas that flow from the
scholar's inclination toward wonder and curiosity. Faculty scholars are indebted to the financial and faith investments of capital-
ists and entrepreneurs and to the vision of civic and political leaders.

One of the more obvious policy accents in American higher
education during the last century was that of access. Americans
more than doubled the number of higher education institutions in
the latter half of the 20th century, built systems of two-year and
community colleges, expanded the number of available graduate
and professional programs, designed massive financial-aid programs, and implemented major federal laws and regulations to
eliminate discrimination related to age, race, gender, and disabil-
ity. The stories of these changes also may be found in our 100
books.

The genius of the American system of education, including its
colleges and universities, is the intent to educate the discretion of

everyone in our society, to call each talent to the far edge of its circle of promise, and thereby create what Benjamin Barber calls *An Aristocracy of Everyone* (1992), a book not on our list but one I might have added in counterpoint to another work that was included, namely William Henry's *In Defense of Elitism* (1994). Henry contends that we have neglected and abandoned points of excellence and standards in favoring our egalitarian impulse. These two works furnish a dialectic about higher education's mission to advance the welfare of individual and society. Here we can feel the sharp edges of the debate concerning higher education's role in advancing the promise of both individual and society, in meeting its personal and civic missions. (Barber's book might have made 101, but then, of course, there would have been a 102 and so on ad infinitum. The line had to be drawn somewhere.)

The policy emphasis on improving access brought into American higher education millions of students from diverse ethnic and economic backgrounds: Asian and Latino students, African Americans and international students, and students from impoverished environments. White student enrollments increased dramatically, and women became the major enrollment class at the undergraduate level and in some graduate and professional fields. This enhanced diversity, however, brought yet another challenge to the "soul" of higher education. Thus you will find in our list of classic works stories of cultural and curriculum contentions over hitherto neglected artistic, religious, and literary traditions from non-European and non-North American cultures and questions on such issues as affirmative action and merit-based admission policies. Is the soul of American higher education to be found in the intellectual traditions, the literature, the art, the history of Western civilization? Or is it to be found in all of the cultures of the world — Asian, Middle Eastern, Native American, African, South American?

We have great expectations — and conflicting expectations — for our colleges and universities. We may claim our colleges and universities as organizing instruments of our curiosity and wonder. We may cherish our colleges and universities as citadels of reason and persuasion. We may profile our colleges and universities as crucibles of dissent and discovery, where we advance on arrogance and prejudice. We may herald our institutions of higher learning as repositories of those things good and beautiful in the human experience. Here is duty of mission extending beyond the facts to the songs that we sing, and a duty to create and maintain cultures of inspiration in music, literature, and the visual and dramatic arts.

I noted earlier that we may consider our colleges and universities as places of paradox, where science and religion live in the same hallway, where cultures of evidence contend with cultures of faith, where the inspiration and influence of religious faith collide with academic freedom and its questioning of dogma. Galileo's facts challenged the Church's power, and science routinely pulls back the curtains of superstition. But faith has built magnificent cathedrals, inspired great music, and produced courageous lives to oppose injustice and totalitarian impulses.

We may mark our colleges and universities as engines of cultural and economic development, as organizations helping both individuals and society realize their full potential. We may assign to them the responsibility of putting knowledge and wisdom to work, laboring in the heated trenches of the nation and the world to battle those problems that beset mind, body, and spirit. The proper work of colleges and universities may be to half soil *and* soul erosion.

Then there is the issue of the pace of change in American higher education. Some corporate and civic voices have lamented the creeping pace of change in American colleges and predicted that these academic dinosaurs will be replaced by cloned versions of proprietary schools, such as the University of Phoenix. To them a black crepe should be hung over the stately arches of our recalcitrant and dying campuses. Thus the effects of new technology constitute still another theme in the unfolding story of higher education's mission. The full story of computer, information, and communications technologies in higher education has not yet been told, but there is sufficient preface in place for us to understand that we may be experiencing serious tectonic shifts in the plates of higher learning. As with the story of past technologies, however, there may be disappointing side-effects to consider as the story unfolds. Issues of quality and integrity are likely to remain paramount.

There is something to be said, however, for the majesty of the andante pace of change. A college or university wavering in the wind to every political breeze, philosophical fad, or methodological whim would not encourage confidence in its stability of mission or thoroughness of method. Nurturing truth and talent is an eminently personal occupation, a work of the long term whose success is not to be found in a neat balance sheet for the current year. It is largely a work of faith and optimism. Students will remember the inspiration of a loving teacher before they will remember numbers and ratios.

Yet another theme in the search for the soul of American higher education concerns the question of governance, the culture of decision and authority in our colleges and universities. This theme is nicely engaged in works by Millett, Mortimer, and Newman in our list of 100 books. If one wants to understand how the political ideology of a society can have a confining effect on the soul of higher education, on the search for truth, then read the story of Russian physicist Sakharov, Russian composer Shostakovich, or Russian writer Solzhenitsyn; consult the chronicles of the 1950s inquiries by Senator Joseph McCarthy in the United States. In a democratic society, scholars and the society must be willing to place perceived truth into the crucible of the public forum, where it may be subjected to intellectual examination and analysis. This public forum test is central to the health of the democratic enterprise. Knowledge becomes not just the servant of the politically or economically powerful but of the saints in the rank and file in our society.

The most obvious feature of American college governance is that decision processes and authority interactions are neither neat nor always easily discerned. In older "tell and compel" versions of leadership in any organization, management folks at the top were viewed as the thinkers; and the folks of the rank and file were viewed as the doers. A college is a place full of thinkers, a place of reverse authority where considerable autonomy is invested in the faculty, a place of shared authority, a place where collegial and consensus decision styles live side by side with bureaucratic and hierarchical structures. Orchestrating complex and competing mission expectations among diverse stakeholders in an authority culture in which consensus and collegiality contend with more directive principles is no small leadership challenge. College administration is no place for amateurs, a theme emphasized in George Keller's *Academic Strategy.*

The rich profile of American higher education institutions, programs, and services today is not the product of timid spirits, empty minds, or dull imaginations, and American management scholar Peter Drucker has cited American universities as a major exemplar of innovation and entrepreneurship.

In an organization that prospects for truth in an adversarial forum, in an organization holding that we have not understood a truth until we have contended with its challenge, we could hardly feel comfortable if our policies and practices, our assumptions and ways of doing business, went unchallenged. The mind of the scholar, therefore, is hospitable to dissent and disputation and should remain so when the dissent and disputation target the heart of the collegiate enterprise.

We must recognize that any organization whose principal work is to assault the limitations of common sense may itself come under assault. Today's truth was yesterday's heresy, and the harbingers of new truth, whether individuals or institutions, are not always greeted with warm embrace. Among those inventive minds we have educated may be one incubating a new vision for American colleges and universities. Thus we might welcome the range and intensity of public criticism directed at the academy as a performance indicator of higher education's success, a "pleasure measure" of some importance and validity.

Are America's colleges and universities to serve as —

- Instruments of personal and societal improvement?
- Crucibles of dissent and discovery?
- Means for transmitting knowledge and culture?
- Conservators of knowledge and heritage?
- Engines of economic development?
- Curators of humankind's artistic impulses?
- Forums for constructing and evaluating public policy?
- Enemies of injustice, ignorance, and arrogance?
- Guardians of human dignity and civility?
- Guarantors of democracy?

In a democratic society, a contentious conversation over higher education purpose and performance is not a sign of pathology but a sign of health and vitality. Dissent over mission and method may be seen as evidence that higher education is meeting its mission responsibility for asking, What is true? What is good? What is beautiful? and for equipping its graduates in both motive and skill to ask penetrating questions, to challenge conventional wisdom, and to ask themselves what brings meaning to their lives and makes them glad to be alive.

Selecting Higher Education's Greatest Hits:
Commentary from the Cutting-Room Floor

by John R. Thelin

Consumer protection agencies continually warn American investors that "if a deal seems too good to be true, it probably is." Although I scrupulously heed this advice with telemarketers and late-night television promotionals for real-estate deals and "vege-matic" devices, I let my guard down with invitations to take on writing projects. The invitation to participate in selecting 100 classic books in higher education stands as Exhibit A.

What started out as a fantastic voyage became a fool's errand. It was the opposite of making nominations for the Hall of Fame. Instead of getting to praise and reward favorite books, the primary task was to delete them. The experience was comparable to a baseball manager making roster cuts at the end of spring training. If these sports analogies fail to make sense, imagine being the airline representative who has the dubious task of telling some ticket holders that their flight is overbooked — and that they will have to give up their seat on the flight. Sorry. Or, to shift from the medium of books to movies, I understand now the sense of loss a filmmaker experiences when one's favorite episode or scene ends up on the cutting-room floor.

We are a nation of list-makers. Lists invariably entice but seldom satisfy. Time and again I tried to identify a conscious or unconscious bias that might be operating in my own nominations or within our group. And then I tried to counter or neutralize it. For example, do we give inordinate, unconscious favor to old works or to recent, familiar ones?

To try to answer that question requires some dissection of the dynamics. First, there is a "tyranny of the majority" even in a group of four. A combination of consensus and popularity often will sand off the sharp edges of memory. For example, I think George Weller's 1932 novel, *Not to Eat, Not for Love,* is the single best depiction of faculty, administrative, and student life within the so-called "modern" university that was taking shape in the 1920s. But my strong conviction means little if none of the other referees have heard of, let alone read, the book. (It wasn't chosen for the list, of course.)

Is the bias of selection tilted toward recent books or toward older works? My hunch is that neither dominates. The preponderance of works are from the recent past — published between about 1955 and 1985. This is understandable because this period coincides with the growth of higher education as a discernible field of scholarship and as an area for doctoral study. Its secondary function is to give strong weight to works written by scholars in the social and behavioral sciences. There still exists a reflex to invoke truly distant works — for example, John Cardinal Newman's *The Idea of a University* — but I believe the canonical list of "war horses" is shrinking both in terms of name recognition and enthusiasm for the nomination. This is healthy. Few higher education scholars today, I suspect, have actually read Newman's "classic work." One reason for my skepticism was learning that the 19th century publisher abandoned the original plan to publish Newman's long series of lectures, mainly because they were tedious and of little interest to the audiences who were supposed to attend them. It's too bad more people have not read Newman closely because it would give good illustrations of how insular, xenophobic, and intolerant thought can be mistakenly exalted into a manifesto of noble vision, especially by those who have not actually read the work.

Although a scattering of contemporary works make the list, my impression is that genuinely new books, published in the past few years, have yet to be read or recognized as "classic." I cite Maresi Nerad's *The Academic Kitchen: A Social History of Gender Stratification at the University of California, Berkeley* (1999) as an example of a memorable, concise work that I think eventually will stand as a classic — but not this time around.

Personal bias works in strange ways. I tend to be the "Typhoid Mary" of books. If I like a title and want to use it in a course, it tends to go out of print. I did have a few titles for which I lobbied shamelessly to include on the list. A.C. Spectorsky's 1958 anthology, *The College Years,* is foremost. Why? First, it is one of the few works that emphasizes fiction, memoirs, autobiography, photographs, and poetry about the American campus — a healthy alternative to our predilection for social and behavioral sciences. Second, it is a memorable, beautiful collection. Third, admittedly a personal bias, it was the book that changed me forever and convinced me that in some vague but enduring way, I wanted to read about and work in higher education — not a bad find in the library stacks on a lonely Saturday night as a college sophomore.

Since the final roster of classics includes annotations, consider this essay an act of loyal dissent. I want to comment on some of my favorite works that "did not make the cut" — as if you hadn't noticed that I've been doing that all along.

Works that combine economic analysis with institutional history and fluid writing hold special appeal. Colin Burke's *American Collegiate Populations: A Test of the Traditional View* (1982) has great worth for me because it is a labor of love. The author spent 10 years in the careful compilations that led to a major reinterpretation of 19th-century American colleges and universities. It is an enduring work because it demonstrated passion combined with persistence and patience. If Colin Burke's macrostatistics leave readers indifferent, how about a consideration of microeconomics and higher education? Margery Somers Foster's 1962 book, *Out of Smalle Beginnings . . . An Economic History of Harvard College in the Puritan Period,* is both outstanding and overlooked. My hypothesis is that the reason this book lapsed from memory is that it was a Greek Tragedy. The Publishing Gods punished the author because the book was "too good for its own good." Stated another way, the research and analysis were so special that anyone reading it would recognize that to incorporate comparable methods and analysis on another era would be demanding and complex. The message, I guess, that has been transmitted to this generation of higher education dissertation writers is that it is better to send out a quick survey on alumni satisfaction.

No doubt the American campus is the obvious focus for most higher education research. The danger of that emphasis is a tendency to gloss over the larger arena of higher education as part of federal and state public policy. I think Chester Finn's 1978 book, *Scholars, Dollars and Bureaucrats,* is conspicuous as a model of significant questions, lively writing, and a combination of political science and history. I kick myself for not having lobbied harder for a work that has the daring to depict the "regulatory swamp" of the federal policy environment.

Clark Kerr's *The Uses of the University* (1963) usually is hailed as the quintessential "great little book." I would like to add to that category another work, also from Berkeley, Earl Cheit's *The Useful Arts and the Liberal Tradition.* Here you have a dean of a business school who devoted himself to persuading faculty from a variety of fields to compare notes and talk to one another. Cheit also found time to teach a course in Berkeley's Graduate School of Education — an endeavor that was the genesis for this delightful, imaginative book that deals with how the "new professions" of business, engineering, agriculture, and forestry each over time found a place at the university table.

Helen Lefkowitz Horowitz has gained attention for her comprehensive interpretation, *Campus Life.* Unfortunate to me, however, is that its popularity overshadows her *Alma Mater*, an innovative work that combines history of campus design with curriculum visions as the theme for a chronological series on the founding of several distinctive women's colleges between 1870 and the 1920s.

Inclusion of Barbara Solomon Miller's *In the Company of Educated Women* is warranted and worthy. However, the trade-off, I fear, is that its comprehensive survey of women and higher education over three centuries may have fulfilled consideration of scholarship about women. I disagree and would liked to have included Geraldine Joncich Clifford's anthology, *Lonely Voyagers,* and Lynn Gordon's *Women and Higher Education in the Progressive Era.*

I am perplexed by the under-representation of works by anthropologists. Michael Moffat's 1989 ethnography of Rutgers freshmen, *Coming of Age in New Jersey*, is high on my list for several reasons: a great title, an imaginative conceptualization, and the incorporation of an under-appreciated discipline into the higher education research arsenal. I am told by colleagues who are "mainline" anthropologists that Moffat's study hardly qualifies as "real anthropology." Nonetheless, it is memorable and imaginative to me. I am sad to report that in polling 25 graduate students in one of my seminars this year, only four read or even heard of Moffat's book. Fame can be fleeting.

I already have indicated my appreciation of memoirs and autobiographies. However, within this genre, works by retired college and university presidents strike me as self-serving and not very interesting. In contrast, Catherine Bateson's *Composing a Life* presents lively, candid insights about campus culture, including a dean's view of Amherst College that upsets the conventional depiction of elite liberal arts college bliss. Richard Rodriguez's *Hunger of Memory* showed how autobiography could simultaneously inform about the world of English departments as well as the experiences of Latino students on the campus and on the academic job market. Henry Seidel Canby's 1936 memoir, *Alma Mater: The Gothic Age of the American College,* may be limited in its appeal to contemporary higher education readers because it relies on Yale as the base on which to build a collective view of campus life in the 1890s. Despite these obvious limits, Canby's ability to reconstruct the details and essence of undergraduate life dispels any doubt about the power of words to move one through time and space. Where then are its sequels and counterparts?

Institutional histories of particular colleges and universities are another paradox in the higher education memory. On the one hand, they are a hardy perennial, especially when a campus wants to commemorate some anniversary, such as a "sesquicentennial." On the other hand, the "house histories" have become a familiar, easy target for serious scholars to shoot down. Given this tendency to dismiss and malign the genre, I wish our list of classic works included Thomas Dyer's remarkable institutional history, *The University of Georgia: A Bicentennial History, 1785-1985* (Athens: University of Georgia Press, 1985). If you want a balanced, thorough account of such episodes and themes as higher education and racial integration or higher education and the place of intercollegiate sports, Dyer's campus history shows by example that the genre need be neither superficial nor ponderous. David Potts' innovative history, *Wesleyan University, 1831-1910: Collegiate Enterprise in New England* (New Haven, Conn.: Yale University Press, 1992), also shows how a thoughtful historian of education can rescue institutional histories from the shoals of predictable chronology and antiquarianism.

Another void in the roster are works dealing expressly with the history of African Americans and higher education. James Anderson's *The Education of Blacks in the South, 1860 to 1935* (1988), has been influential. Probably it does not fare well in the higher education category because its scope extends to a broad treatment of social and education analysis. In a similar vein, Robert Eng's *Black Hampton* is more likely to be nominated if the criteria were local history and community studies rather than "higher education" *per se*. I would say, however, that I have not yet encountered a history of historically black colleges and universities that strikes me as truly memorable and enduring.

The community college as a distinct institution is underrepresented. Two works I would consider as classics are Howard London's *The Culture of a Community College* and Jerome Brinton and David Karrabel's *The Diverted Dream*. Each goes beyond the conventional liturgy of celebration and succeeds in making the community college part of the fabric of America's higher education tapestry.

I like coffee table books and photographic essays about campuses. Granted, these are not the stuff of which graduate seminar discussions or experimental design research studies are made. But they have an important place in our heritage. Perhaps a good compromise might have been to include the photographic essay that Oliver Jensen edited and wrote for *American Heritage* magazine in 1974: *A College Album: Or, Rah, Rah, Yesterday!*

About six years ago Alexander Astin wrote a back-page essay for the *Chronicle of Higher Education* in which he discussed "moving target research." His concept intrigued me. It also made me reflect on my own experiences in higher education as a field of scholarship. In contrast to Astin's "moving target," my graduate students have from time to time suggested that I am a fixture. The notes I used to teach "Contemporary Issues in Higher Education" in 1974 now qualify as material for lectures on the "History of Higher Education." Time has moved forward while my lectures have remained constant. Perhaps this gives higher education research some appeal for its efficient recycling of data. It also suggests that each of us has a time and timing, subject to a few strengths and many limits. Given my limits, the residual influence this project and essay have had on me is my recognition that I am especially excited about the nominations and discussions about higher education books by a new, vital generation of graduate students and scholars.

Title Index

About the Authors

CAMERON FINCHER is regents professor of higher education and psychology at the University of Georgia, where, for 30 years until 1999, he also was director of the Institute of Higher Education. Formerly he was a professor of psychology at Georgia State University in Atlanta and directed testing and counseling services. A graduate of the University of Georgia, he earned his M.A. at the University of Minnesota and a Ph.D. at Ohio State University.

Fincher's teaching and research have been devoted to leadership, education policy, and evaluation and assessment. He has served on numerous commissions and task forces in these areas. His many articles have been published in psychology journals, such as *American Psychologist* and *Personnel Psychology;* education journals, such as *Educational Researcher, College Board Review,* and *Research in Higher Education;* and others periodicals, such as *Atlanta Economic Review.*

Fincher has received several awards for his work, including the College Board's Ben Gibson Award for outstanding contributions to education, the Sidney Suslow Award from the Association for Institutional Research, and the Howard R. Bowen Distinguished Career Award from the Association for the Study of Higher Education.

GEORGE KELLER is an education consultant, a scholar of higher education, and an award-winning editor, writer, and strategic planner. After earning his undergraduate and graduate degrees at Columbia University, he served there as a faculty member and a dean. He later worked as a presidential assistant for the State University of New York system and for the University of Maryland system, before chairing the program in higher education studies at the University of Pennsylvania's Graduate School of Education.

The author of more than 100 articles and reviews and author of three books, including *Academic Strategy*, Keller also edited the journal, *Planning for Higher Education,* from 1990 to 1997. He has consulted at more than 120 colleges, universities, and state systems in the United States and abroad. Among his awards are the U.S. Steel Foundation Medal for "distinguished service to higher education" and the Founders Award from the Society for College and University Planning for "distinguished achievement in the field of education planning."

E. GRADY BOGUE is a professor of educational leadership and policy studies at the University of Tennessee. He is also chancellor emeritus of Louisiana State University in Shreveport and a former chief academic officer for the Tennessee Higher Education Commission, where he designed the nation's first state-level performance incentive program for higher education.

Bogue received his B.S. degree in mathematics in 1957 from the University of Memphis. He served as an instructor of electronics with the U.S. Air Force and of physics with the U.S. Navy before returning to the University of Memphis to earn his doctorate in education and to work there as an administrator. He has been an ACE Fellow and a visiting scholar at the Educational Testing Service, and he consults for colleges and state-level agencies.

Bogue is the author of six books, the latest of which is *Exploring the Heritage of American Higher Education* (Oryx Press, 2000) and has published more than 50 articles in periodicals, such as *Journal of Higher Education* and the *Harvard Business Review.*

JOHN R. THELIN is a professor of history of higher education and public policy at the University of Kentucky and recent president of the Association for the Study of Higher Education

(ASHE). Previously he was a professor of higher education and philanthropy at Indiana University and chancellor professor at the College of William and Mary, where he also served as president of the faculty senate and received the Phi Beta Kappa Award for outstanding faculty contribution to scholarship.

A graduate of Brown University, he earned an M.A. in American History and a Ph.D. in the History of Education at the University of California, Berkeley. Thelin is the author of five books, including *Games Colleges Play*, a history of intercollegiate sports and reform attempts, and more than 60 articles in such publications as the *Wall Street Journal* and the *Chronicle of Higher Education* and such scholarly journals as the *Review of Higher Education* and *Educational Studies*. He currently is conducting a study of research universities in the South, aided by a Spencer Foundation grant.